Official guide to Hiking *the* Grand Canyon

by Scott Thybony

With contributions to the *Leave No Trace* and *Planning a Safe Trip* chapters
by Sam West and Mark Sinclair.

ISBN 0-938216-48-1   LCN 94-075571

editing
Pam Frazier

design & illustration
Larry Lindahl

trail profile research
Michelle McIntyre

geologic cross section
John Dawson

photography credits
Arizona Historical Society, W. W. Bass Collection: p. 57 (top);
Tom Bean: pp. iii, 4, 6, 10, 31, 35, 53 (top), 59;
Art Brown: p. 46;
Mike Buchheit: p. 59 (bottom);
C. J. Crossland: p. 15 (top);
Richard Danley: pp. 12, 52, 53 (bottom);
George H.H. Huey: p. 57 (bottom);
Kolb Brothers, Emery Kolb Collection, Cline Library,
Nothern Arizona University, Flagstaff, AZ: pp. 56 (NAU 568-5501),
63 (NAU 568-6151), 65 (NAU 568-5384);
Gary Ladd: p. 2;
Larry Lindahl: front cover, pp. i, iv, 9, 21, 26, 27 (both);
Museum of Northern Arizona: p. 48;
National Park Service: pp. 39, 61.

www.grandcanyon.org

CONTENTS

"I envision
national parks as ...
models of respect
for all land and water
and all of life."

MICHAEL FROME

INTRODUCTION

"Now I see the secret of making the best
persons, it is to grow in the open air and
to eat and sleep with the earth."

WALT WHITMAN

T HIS GUIDEBOOK presents an overview of the major
trails in the Grand Canyon. It provides basic
information needed to plan an inner canyon hike
or a walk on the rim. It doesn't cover every turn of the
trail and is not intended to be used for route finding.
Detailed guides to individual trails are available for the
most popular hikes; other guidebooks focus on off-trail
routes (see *Suggested Reading* list at the end of this book).

Trails, and the roads leading to them, change over
time. Check with the park rangers for current information
when obtaining backcountry permits. Keep in mind that
a guidebook is no substitute for proper planning, good
physical condition, and solid judgment.

*Sunrise from Hopi
Point, South Rim.*

LEAVE NO TRACE

Hiker and ocotillo wands near mouth of Havasu Canyon.

IN RECENT YEARS the Grand Canyon has experienced a dramatic increase in visitation and, with it, increased backcountry use.

While you, the backpacker, are part of a small percentage of the total park visitation, you have the greatest potential for damaging the canyon's fragile desert environment. Littered trails and campsites, improperly buried fecal matter, polluted water sources, denuded vegetation, fire scars, and unnecessary multiple trailing systems bear witness to the presence of human beings and the vulnerability of the resources.

Fortunately, along with increased visitation in ·the backcountry, a strong minimum-impact ethic has developed toward its use. Without it, the wilderness experience itself is threatened with extinction. Everything you do in the wilderness—your route, your gear, choosing your campsite—should reflect a commitment to "leave no trace." Looking closely and thinking carefully will allow you to assess potential human impact in any given situation and adjust your behavior accordingly. The right attitude will do more to preserve the wilderness than any number of rules and regulations. When you leave the canyon, there should be no trace that you have been there.

If you are already familiar with the tenets of minimum-impact backpacking, we still ask that you carefully read the following information. Several of the techniques are unique to a desert environment and differ considerably from those you would use in an alpine setting.

We also ask you to remember that Grand Canyon National Park has a permit system to protect the integrity of the wilderness and your experience in it. For the sake of the wilderness, respect the system and adhere to the itinerary outlined on your permit. Most backcountry use occurs during the spring and summer months and around holidays. To lessen impact on the canyon (and avoid the extreme heat of summer), consider planning your trip for the off-season.

■ CAMPSITE SELECTION

Select your campsite with care. Use designated campsites where they are provided or choose places that have been camped in previously. You will have the least impact if you choose sites with an absence of vegetation and organic soil. Sandy areas, dry washes, and slickrock benches make the best campsites. However, be aware of the danger of flash flooding in dry washes during the late summer months or at any time when rain or runoff are possible.

All campsites should be located at least 100 feet (30 m) from water sources to prevent pollution of this limited and life-sustaining resource and to allow unobstructed access for wildlife. Avoid making campsite "improvements." Trenching around tents, vegetation removal, soil disturbance, and the building of rock or wood shelters are all visible signs of your presence. Think about it: wouldn't you rather encounter undisturbed wilderness than the remains of another person's camp? You might also consider, particularly when camped in the vicinity of others, that everything from the noise you make to the color of your equipment has an impact on the solitude and quality of the wilderness experience.

■ FIRES

No open fires are allowed while backpacking in the canyon due to the shortage of wood and the danger of wildfires. Besides, the remains of a fire are an eyesore. Charcoal and ash can take hundreds of years to break down in this arid climate. They have accumulated in many backcountry areas and turned the native soil a dirty grey. Flames have blackened rock walls that are millions of years old.

"Though we travel the world over to find the beautiful, we must carry it with us or we find it not."

RALPH
WALDO
EMERSON

Use lightweight backpacking stoves for cooking; they will cook your food faster than an open fire, leaving more time for you to enjoy the canyon. Keep your meals simple and light. This will cut down on the weight you carry in and the garbage you will have to carry out. During the hot summer months, most experienced canyon hikers carry meals that require no cooking.

The Southwestern sky is awe-inspiring at night; don't detract from it with an illegal fire.

■ *TRAIL USE & ROUTE SELECTION*

Remain on designated trails wherever they are provided. Cutting switchbacks damages trails and is unsafe for you and hikers that might be below you. In many areas hikers have established multiple trails in the same general locales. These unnecessary trails result in erosion, destruction of soil composition, and trampling of delicate vegetation. Avoid adding to this confusing network of parallel or undesignated footpaths.

"The people walk over me. The old men say to me, I am beautiful."

NAVAJO CHANT

Tonto Trail near Hermit Canyon.

When exploring off trail, walk single file and make your route over slickrock, in dry washes, or through sandy and unvegetated areas. Be careful not to disturb fragile ground cover that prevents erosion. It can take a hundred years for soil and vegetation to recover from human impact.

■ HUMAN WASTE

This is the greatest problem in the Grand Canyon backcountry, because human waste decomposes very slowly in the relatively sterile desert soil. Use toilets where they are provided. In wilderness areas where they are not available, deposit feces at least 100 feet (30 m) from trails, campsites, and water sources. Choose an area with richer, darker soil. Then dig a small hole about six inches (15 cm) deep, disturbing the soil as little as possible. Make your deposit and cover it with the soil you have just removed.

Pack out all your toilet paper in plastic bags with your other trash rather than burning or burying it. Many wildfires in the canyon have been started by burning trash and toilet paper.

■ CARE OF WATER SOURCES

Never wash clothes, dishes, or yourself directly in a water source. Instead, carry water at least 100 feet (30 m) from the source in a clean container. Be sure to use biodegradable soap. Dirty water should be dispersed in vegetated soil—again, well removed from the water supply. Conserve water whenever possible. Other hikers and wildlife in this arid environment may depend on it for survival.

You should also remember that other hikers and wildlife may have polluted water sources. Purify all water taken from natural sources by using iodine or bleach, or by boiling or filtering it.

■ LITTER

Whatever you carry into the wilderness you must carry out. Nothing should be left or buried in the backcountry, including food scraps, wet garbage, grease, and cigarette butts. These substances will take years to decompose in a desert climate. Food particles that are left behind will cause increased populations of flies, ants, and rodents. More than one backpacker has awakened to find that varmints have torn holes in their new pack and eaten or contaminated their remaining food. Suspend all food-sacks freehanging above the ground.

All of us must take pride in leaving the Grand Canyon cleaner than we found it.

"The greatest good you can do for the canyon is to leave no trace that you have been here."

BACKCOUNTRY
RANGER

■ WILDLIFE & WILDFLOWERS

The canyon is home to a variety of plants and animals. While not frequently seen, some, like the rattlesnakes and scorpions, may create problems for the unaware hiker. Appreciate the danger and beauty of these canyon dwellers and do not disturb them.

Desert plants and flowers can take hundreds of years to grow back after being damaged. The flower you pick may be the only one that plant has produced in years. Take a picture and leave the plant. You should also be aware that many species of desert plants concentrate poisonous minerals from the soil in their stems and leaves. The canyon is not a good place to experiment with eating wild foods.

■ INDIAN RUINS & MINING CAMPS

Ancient granaries near Nankoweap.

More than 2000 ruins of prehistoric Indian dwellings dot the Grand Canyon. There are also numerous nineteenth-century mining camps. Archaeological and historic sites in the canyon are non-renewable and, unlike some other resources, can never be replaced.

If you come upon some of these sites while backpacking, treat them with care. Don't set up camp in these ruins or walk on the walls. Leave any pottery (even broken pieces) or arrow points where you find them. Remember that for the archaeologist, context or association is as important as the object itself. Moving a piece of pottery even a few yards may render it useless in determining how these ancient canyon dwellers lived.

Once again, federal and state laws protect these sites for future generations to study and enjoy, but the best guarantee of their preservation is a respect for the Grand Canyon and its history.

We hope that you will find these suggestions and techniques helpful on your trek into the canyon wilderness. They are not meant so much to regulate or control your experience as to enhance it. The lighter you travel, the less each step you take impacts the earth. The more closely you observe the land in attempting to have a minimal impact on it, the more you will see. The more conscious you become of the vulnerable and interrelated aspects of the canyon's environment, the better are the chances that it will remain unchanged for coming generations. Walk softly.

PLANNING A SAFE TRIP

WARNING

E ACH YEAR park rangers conduct hundreds of search and rescue efforts (at evacuee's expense) within the Grand Canyon. They find hikers suffering from the heat, others who have run out of water, some who have fallen off cliffs, a few who have drowned in the river.

Good planning is essential for a safe trip into a rugged canyon environment with extreme high and low temperatures and little shade or water. The decisions you make have life-or-death consequences.

HAZARDS

■ TEMPERATURE EXTREMES

HEAT. Inner canyon temperatures during summer consistently exceed 100° F (38° C) and sometimes top 115° F (46° C) in the shade. Heat increases as you descend into the gorge. Temperatures on the canyon floor average 20 to 30 degrees warmer than the rims. Heat and the lack of shade greatly reduce a hiker's efficiency—you may be able to cover only half the distance you could under normal conditions.

Avoid overheating your body. During summer, stay in the shade during the midday heat. Hike during the cool of early morning, late afternoon, and at night if necessary. Wear a hat and clothing that covers the body. Drink plenty of water and eat salty snacks. Consider avoiding the inner canyon heat by hiking along the rim trails.

Plan trips for the cooler seasons. Spring and fall are usually the most comfortable times to hike in the Grand Canyon. But even then the weather is unpredictable.

COLD. Be prepared for snowfall on the rims any time between September and June. During winter packed snow and ice may cover the upper sections of Grand Canyon trails. Experienced hikers take instep crampons for traction on slick trails and carry ski poles to use as walking sticks.

Winter temperatures often drop below freezing, and the weather can be extremely variable. If it is snowing on

"As long as there are canyons, people will be drawn to them."

ANONYMOUS

7

the rim, it may be raining at the river. Consider taking a tent or bivouac sack. A long-sleeve shirt may be enough one day, but you may need rain gear and a heavy parka on the next. Many hikers prefer to wear synthetic "warm when wet" fabrics for cold-weather hiking.

Common weather-related emergencies are *heat exhaustion, heat stroke,* and *hypothermia.* Beware of these potential problems and prevent them whenever possible.

HEAT EXHAUSTION is usually caused by physical exertion during prolonged exposure to heat.

Symptoms: Headache, moist and clammy skin, weakness, dizziness, pupils dilated, normal or subnormal body temperature, possible vomiting.

Treatment: Rest in cool, shaded area. Wet victim's clothing and have victim lie down with feet elevated. Let the person drink an electrolyte replacement drink such as Gatorade™, ERG™, or Gookinade™. *Get help.*

HEAT STROKE is less common but *far more serious.* The victim may die if proper treatment is not given. Heat stroke is normally caused by a failure in the person's sweating mechanism causing the body to overheat during exertion. Treatment is aimed at ridding the body of excess heat.

Symptoms: Dry, hot skin; very high body temperature; dry armpits; possible unconsciousness.

Treatment: Cool the body immediately—get victim into shade, fan the body, and sponge with or immerse in water. *Remember, the victim may die unless you actively work at lowering his or her body temperature. Get help immediately.*

HYPOTHERMIA, or "freezing to death," is caused by exposure to cold, wet, or windy conditions. Most cases develop in air temperatures between 30° and 50° F (-1° and 10° C).

Prevention: Stay dry, beware of wind, understand cold and what it can do to you.

Symptoms: Persistent or violent shivering; vague, slow and slurred speech; frequent stumbling; exhaustion; memory lapses; incoherence; poor judgement.

Treatment: Get out of the wind and rain, get into dry clothing, give victim warm drinks, and place him or her in a dry sleeping bag. If symptoms are advanced, try to

"Brute force without wisdom falls by its own weight."

HORACE

keep victim awake and get into the sleeping bag with them. Skin-to-skin contact is the most effective way to supply heat.

■ *THIRST*

Dehydration occurs quickly in the arid conditions encountered below the rim. Hikers lose ½ quart to 1½ quarts of water per hour on average through sweat and expiration, and can lose up to 3 quarts per hour.

In the desert water is life. Carry *at least* 4 quarts of water per person per day on summer hikes. If walking in the heat of day, you may need more. Pay attention to water intake. Estimate needs by urine output; volume and color should remain normal. If you don't feel like drinking or eating, rest until you do. Purify water taken from potholes, creeks, and the Colorado River. Consider stashing water on the way in for use on the way out.

Avoid water intoxication (hyponatremia), an electrolyte imbalance caused by drinking plenty of water but eating too little food. Plan on eating three meals a day and snacking often between meals. Many canyon hikers carry electrolyte drinks (Gookinade™, ERG™, Gatorade™). And remember to travel light—the heaviest item in your pack should be water.

■ *TERRAIN*

Hikers descend into a cliff-enclosed wilderness on steep trails that can be grueling—all downhill on the way in and all uphill on the return. Canyon hiking is the opposite of mountain climbing. The difficult climb and the thin air of the higher elevations come at the end of the hike when you are already tired.

PACE YOURSELF. Know your limits. Take it slow at first and avoid blisters by applying Band-Aids™ or moleskin to "hot spots." Allow twice as much time for hiking out as hiking in. First-time canyon hikers average 1 mile an hour going uphill.

DON'T HIKE ALONE. Groups should stay together. Don't let a slower member fall behind, and never leave a sick or injured hiker alone. Keep the most experienced hikers in the front and rear of the party. Hiking alone increases the risk of serious trouble.

Switchbacks in "The Chimney" at the top of South Kaibab Trail.

PLAN AHEAD. Do not attempt to walk from rim to river and back in a single day. Distance is deceiving. The clear, dry air of the desert makes things look closer than they are. Hikers can easily overextend themselves. Take a flashlight and extra food and water on day hikes.

The most common terrain-related emergencies are fractures and accompanying shock. Hikers should also be aware of these symptoms and the current treatments for these problems.

Descending the Nankoweap Trail, North Rim.

GETTING HELP. Do not leave the injured party alone if this can be avoided. Be prepared to send a member of the group or ask a passerby to get help for you. The messenger should carry a description of the injuries, the treatment given, the precise location of the injured party, the victim's age, gender, and weight, and any medications the person may be taking. It is an excellent idea to mark the location of an injured party on your topographic map before you go for help. Evacuation will probably be made by helicopter, and much of the canyon looks the same from the air.

Corridor-trail ranger stations are located at Indian Garden and Bright Angel Campground year-round, and at Cottonwood Campground during the summer. Emergency phones are located at several points along the corridor trails.

■ ISOLATION

The Grand Canyon is a vast, roadless wilderness covering almost 2000 square miles. Help may not reach an injured hiker for days. Even in the main cross-canyon corridor aid will not be immediate. Carry—and know how to use—a compass, a topographic map, and a signal mirror. Even day hikers should inform someone of their itinerary.

If you should become lost, try to retrace your steps to where you left the trail. If all attempts to find a point of reference fail, sit down and collect your thoughts.

STAY IN ONE PLACE; you will be found more quickly. Use your signal mirror to attract the attention of passing aircraft or, if in view, signal to people on the rim. If you leave to get water or for some other reason, leave a note telling where you went and include the time and date. Return to the area as quickly as possible.

MAKE A LARGE "X" on the ground using your clothing and gear.

■ OTHER HAZARDS

BITES, STINGS, AND PUNCTURES. Rattlesnake bites are rare—most occur when people try to handle the snakes. Scorpion stings happen more frequently. Although painful, they rarely cause serious medical problems. Shake out sleeping bags and check boots and clothing before dressing. Wear shoes in camp and inspect wood and rocks before lifting. Red ant bites can be painful. Avoid nests and keep from spilling food. The tips of cactus and agave spines can give painful punctures. Keep alert, especially when hiking off the trail.

Scorpion.

RIVER AND FLASH FLOODS. Flash floods can appear with little warning. Under a clear sky, a wall of water fed by runoff from a distant rainstorm can suddenly rip down a normally dry wash. Avoid camping in dry washes whenever flooding or runoff threaten.

Do not attempt to swim in the Colorado River. Powerful currents and bitter cold water (45-50° F/7-10° C) have taken numerous lives.

CANYON HIKING

O'Neill Butte from Cedar Ridge, South Kaibab Trail.

Split-twig figurine.

HUNTERS FIRST ENTERED the Grand Canyon on foot thousands of years ago. They followed game trails into the gorge, leaving ritual offerings in caves and painting visionary images on cliff walls. Other Indians followed them, farming scattered pockets of arable land. Native cultures have occupied the area more or less continuously since that time; today the Paiute, Hualapai, and Havasupai Indians still make the canyons and plateaus their home.

During the late nineteenth-century, prospectors, cattlemen, and scientists improved the old footpaths for horse and burro. Today a widespread network of trails, many abandoned more than half a century ago, crisscross the park. They range from faint traces to broad, well-maintained thoroughfares—*but no trail is easy.*

An early traveler once asked a prospector how to get to the Colorado River. "Well," he answered, "there's only two ways that I know of. You have a choice between the hard way and the harder way."

Trails are not rated since their difficulty varies from season to season and from hiker to hiker. Contributing factors include weather, time of day, and a hiker's physical condition and experience.

First-time hikers should keep to the "corridor trails"— that is, the Bright Angel and North and South Kaibab Trails. Next, try the Hermit, Grandview, or Clear Creek Trails. Once you have gained experience, sample the South Bass, New Hance, Thunder River, and Tanner Trails. Of the major trails, the Boucher, North Bass, and Nankoweap are generally considered the most challenging.

■ TRAIL CATEGORIES

CORRIDOR TRAIL. National Park Service personnel regularly maintain and frequently patrol these wide, well-marked trails. These trails—the Bright Angel and the North and South Kaibab—comprise the main cross-canyon corridor, the most popular backcountry use area.

WILDERNESS TRAIL. These secondary trails are no longer regularly maintained and are less frequently patrolled. Many are narrow footpaths that require some route-finding ability and occasional scrambling. Water sources are scarce and unreliable. Maps and prior Grand Canyon hiking experience are recommended.

ROUTE. Seldom patrolled and often difficult to follow, these off-trail routes follow natural breaks in the terrain. Often obliterated by rockslides and brush, they may require exposed climbs. Detailed maps and route-finding ability are essential, and water sources are limited. All but the most experienced canyon hikers should avoid hiking in these conditions.

■ MAPS

U.S. Geological Survey topographic maps (15 minute and 7.5 minute quadrangles) are the standard maps for Grand Canyon hiking. The newer 7.5' series maps show more detail and are especially helpful for off-trail hiking. The Kaibab National Forest road map for the North Kaibab Ranger District is useful for finding distant North Rim trailheads. See pages 66 and 67 for selected maps and trail guides that are available from Grand Canyon Association, 520-638-2481.

"Of what avail are forty freedoms without a blank spot on the map?"

ALDO
LEOPOLD

You don't need to hike to the river to experience the Grand Canyon. Day hiking can be extremely rewarding. You may wish to venture a ways into the canyon or stay on the cooler shaded rims where, even during the busiest season, it is easy to escape the crowds.

Recommendations for day hikes can be found at the beginning of the sections describing trails on the South and North Rims, and day-hike destinations into the canyon are indicated on the trail profiles that accompany maps. If you decide to go into the canyon, keep track of the time and remember that it will take you twice as long to hike out as it did to hike in.

Permits are not required for day hikes, but it's a good idea to inform someone of your plans, even if you don't intend to leave the rim.

■ *OVERNIGHT HIKING*

Permits are required for all overnight use of the back-country (see *Permits* below).

Established campgrounds in the main corridor are located along the Bright Angel and North Kaibab Trails. In more remote areas with heavy use, regulations limit camping to designated campsites. At-large camping is permitted in other use areas. Check with the Backcountry Information Center for current camping restrictions.

PERMITS

Park regulations *require* permits for all overnight back-country hiking within Grand Canyon and undeveloped areas on the rims. They have established a permit system to lessen congestion and prevent overuse of the canyon wilderness.

There is a charge for permits, which are issued on a first-come, first-served basis. Because of the tremendous demand for permits, hikers need to obtain permits by mail, fax, or in person no more than four months in advance. If permit requests are made a month or more in advance, the permit will be mailed to the trip leader. Requests made less than a month in advance may not be processed in time for a mail response.

If you do not receive a permit before traveling, you must pick up your permit between 8 a.m. and 5 p.m.

"Not in the clamour of the street, not in the shouts and plaudits of the throng, but in ourselves, are triumph and defeat."

HENRY
WORDSWORTH
LONGFELLOW

Camp on Tanner Trail below Desert View Watchtower.

Mountain Standard Time on the day before or the day your trip begins. Permits may be claimed at the Backcountry Information Center located in Grand Canyon Village at the Maswik Transportation Center, or at the North Rim Backcountry Office when the North Rim is open (mid-May to mid-October).

Hiking permits also may be obtained at Pipe Springs National Monument and at the Bureau of Land Management office in St. George, Utah. Permits may sometimes be obtained from rangers on duty at the Tuweep, Meadview, and Lees Ferry Ranger Stations. However, these rangers have other patrol responsibilities and may not be available to provide assistance.

Hikers who arrive without advance permits may place their names on a waiting list for cancellations.

Contact the Backcountry Information Center for a Trip Planning Packet and Permit Request Form. Park rangers do not accept permit requests over the phone.

BACKCOUNTRY INFORMATION CENTER
Grand Canyon National Park
P.O. Box 129, Grand Canyon, AZ 86023-0129
www.nps.gov/grca   Fax: 520-638-2125

You may also call the Backcountry Information Center at 520-638-7875 weekdays (except holidays) between 1 p.m. and 5 p.m. M.S.T. Recorded information on trail conditions and additional permit information is available 24 hours a day at 520-638-7888.

GENERAL INFORMATION

■ CLIMATE

Average temperatures (°F) and precipitation:

	South Rim			Inner Gorge			North Rim		
	Max	Min	Precip	Max	Min	Precip	Max	Min	Precip
January	41°	18°	1.32"	56°	36°	.68"	37°	16°	3.17"
April	60°	32°	.93"	82°	56°	.47"	53°	29°	1.73"
July	84°	54°	1.81"	106°	78°	.84"	77°	46°	1.93"
October	65°	36°	1.10"	84°	58°	.65"	59°	31°	1.38"

■ PHANTOM RANCH

Located at the bottom of the Grand Canyon near the Colorado River, this guest ranch provides meals, cabins, and dormitory accommodations for mule riders and hikers. Advance reservations are required. Contact AmFac Parks & Resorts, 14001 E. Iliff, Aurora, CO 80014, 303-297-2757.

■ FISHING

A current Arizona fishing license and trout stamp are required for fishing within the park. A license may be obtained at Canyon Village Marketplace on the South Rim.

■ PETS

Pets are not allowed below the rim. Failure to comply results in a costly fine. Grand Canyon National Park Lodges operates a pet kennel on the South Rim only. Information and boarding arrangements may be made by calling 520-638-0534.

■ BICYCLES

Bicycles are prohibited from all trails in Grand Canyon National Park, including the rim trails. Bicycles are allowed on all paved and unpaved roads in the park.

■ HAVASUPAI INDIAN RESERVATION

The National Park Service does not make reservations or issue hiking permits for the Havasupai Indian Reservation. These must be obtained through Havasupai Tribal Enterprises, Supai, AZ 86435, 520-448-2141.

"There's a long, long trail a-winding into the land of my dreams."

STODDARD KING

THE HIKING TRAILS

TRAIL CONDITIONS

Corridor Trail. National Park Service personnel regularly maintain and frequently patrol these wide, well-marked trails. These trails—the Bright Angel and the North and South Kaibab—comprise the main cross-canyon corridor, the most popular backcountry use area.

Wilderness Trail. These secondary trails are no longer regularly maintained and are less frequently patrolled. Many are narrow footpaths that require some route-finding ability and occasional scrambling. Water sources are scarce and unreliable.

Route. Seldom patrolled and often difficult to follow, these off-trail routes follow natural breaks in the terrain. Often obliterated by rockslides and brush, they may require exposed climbs. Route-finding ability is essential, and water sources are limited. All but the most experienced canyon hikers should avoid hiking in these conditions. Routes are not covered in this book.

ABOUT THE TRAIL PROFILES

Trail profiles have been prepared with a vertical (elevation) exaggeration of 1.5x; the horizontal (distance) axis is not exaggerated. Allow for a statistical error of approximately 40 feet (12 m). Suggested day-hike destinations are indicated on the profiles.

ABOUT THE MAPS

The maps in this book are provided for planning purposes only. They are not intended for route-finding in the backcountry. We recommend that you obtain detailed topographic maps of the area in which you will be hiking before entering the backcountry. Appropriate U.S.G.S. topographic maps are listed at the beginning of individual trail descriptions.

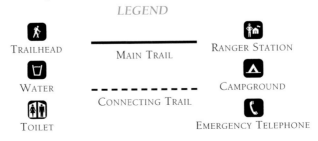

LEGEND

TRAILHEAD   MAIN TRAIL   RANGER STATION

WATER   CONNECTING TRAIL   CAMPGROUND

TOILET   EMERGENCY TELEPHONE

KAIBAB

NATIONAL

FOREST

Great Thumb

Mesa

G R A N D   C A N Y O N

COLORADO

Elves Chasm

South Bass

Tonto

HAVASUPAI

INDIAN

RESERVATION

Boucher   **Hermit**

Hermit

Hermits Rest

Waldron

NOTE: Shaded relief is an artistic rendering and is not accurate in detail. Simplified trails are shown for orientation purposes only, and are not intended for route finding in the field.

↑ to Jacob Lake and Kanab

↑ to Lees Ferry

SOUTH RIM TRAILS

N
W E
S

NAVAJO

INDIAN

RESERVATION

Park Entrance

Point Imperial

NATIONAL   PARK

Little Colorado River

Grand Canyon Lodge

Beamer

North Kaibab

Cape Royal

Phantom Ranch

Clear Creek

Canyon View Information Plaza

Escalante

South Kaibab

Desert View

RIVER

Grand Canyon Village

Tonto

Tanner

Tusayan Ruins

Desert View Drive

Grandview

New Hance

Park Entrance

64

64

64

↓ to Williams and Flagstaff

KAIBAB   NATIONAL   FOREST

to Cameron ↘

SOUTH RIM TRAILS

HIKING ALONG THE RIM

T RAILS WIND ALONG the brink of the Grand Canyon on the South Rim through pinyon-juniper forests. These pathways lead to panoramic viewpoints of the inner canyon and distant views of the river. They offer less strenuous hiking, cooler temperatures, and more shade than the inner canyon trail system. No permits are needed for day hiking.

ALONG THE SOUTH RIM
SHORTER TRAILS

Tusayan Ruin Walk: 0.2 miles (0.32 km)
This short trail winds through the remains of a prehistoric Pueblo structure near Desert View Drive. The trail is paved, and wheelchair-accessible with assistance. A self-guiding trail brochure is available at the trailhead. The adjacent Tusayan Museum features exhibits about the people who occupied the ruin site some 800 years ago, and the museum's bookstore offers relevant publications.

Striking Out on Your Own
Canyon overlooks and picnic sites along Desert View Drive offer parking for impromptu walks along the canyon rim or through the forest. Hikers may find solitude within yards of these parking areas. However, be advised that no formal trails exist and footing can be dangerous. Please use caution along the rim and choose your path carefully to protect vegetation and other natural features.

ALONG THE SOUTH RIM
RIM TRAIL

Length
• 9 miles (14 km): Hermits Rest to Mather Point
  Hike all or part.

Maps:

Bright Angel (15 minute)

Phantom Ranch and Grand Canyon (7.5 minute)

Elevations
• 6640 feet (2024 m): Hermits Rest
• 7120 feet (2170 m): Mather Point

Water Sources
• Hermits Rest
• Grand Canyon Village
• Yavapai Point
• Canyon View Information Plaza

Trail Conditions
Paved trail for 3.5 miles (5.6 km) between Maricopa and Yavapai points; dirt footpath the remainder of the way.

Generally level, the steepest section lies west of Grand Canyon Village where the trail ascends an uplifted section of the Bright Angel Fault. There are no protective railings along most of the trail.

Trailhead

The Rim Trail can be reached from the major viewpoints and pulloffs along Hermit Road and Village Loop Drive. The shuttle bus stops at viewpoints from Hermits Rest to Mather Point.

Route

The pathway heading east from Hermits Rest winds through pinyon pine, juniper, and thickets of Gambel oak. Passing Pima Point, it hugs the edge of the 3000-foot (914 m) precipice known as The Abyss and loops out to Mohave and Hopi Points. Hopi Point offers views for 45 miles (72.4 km) up and down the canyon.

Just before reaching Maricopa Point the trail passes the Powell Memorial. Major John Wesley Powell led the first expedition to traverse the Colorado River through the Grand Canyon in 1869. Navajo Indians once lit signal fires on Powell Point, relayed by other fires at Desert View and in the Painted Desert beyond.

The paved trail follows the west side of Bright Angel Canyon and descends to the head of Bright Angel Trail and Grand Canyon Village. The trail enters the Village Historic District, passing buildings such as the Kolb Studio, Bright Angel Lodge, and El Tovar Hotel. Grand Canyon Village grew up around the railway that reached the South Rim in 1901.

Mather Point is named for Stephen Mather, first director of the National Park Service.

Continuing east, the trail reaches Yavapai Observation Station and Mather Point. Mather Point is named for Stephen T. Mather, first director of the National Park Service. An unimproved path heads east another 2.5 miles (4 km) to connect with the South Kaibab trailhead at Yaki Point.

Interpretive brochures are available in boxes at several locations along the trail.

SOUTH BASS TRAIL

Maps:

*Havasupai Point
(15 minute)*

*Havasupai Point
(7.5 minute)*

*Archaeological
evidence shows that
prehistoric Cohonina
Indians used this
route, followed in
more recent times by
Havasupai Indians.*

*Canyon pioneer
William Bass
improved the Indian
footpaths for horse-
back travel. Bass
developed a tourist
camp on the South
Rim and a winter
camp and mines on
the north side of the
Colorado River.*

*Initially, he guided
sightseers across the
river by boat and
then by cable crossing
(now dismantled) to
reach his trail leading
to the North Rim.*

*To do the laundry
during dry spells,
his wife, Ada Bass,
would bundle up the*

Length
- about 7.8 miles (12.6 km): South Bass trailhead to the Colorado River

Elevations
- 6650 feet (2027 m): South Bass trailhead
- 2250 feet (686 m): Colorado River

Water Source
- Colorado River

Trail Conditions
Wilderness Trail. Washouts require some route-finding ability.

Trailhead
South Bass Trail begins about 31 miles (49.9 km) west of Grand Canyon Village via Rowe Well Road and Forest Service Road 328. A Kaibab National Forest map is recommended to avoid becoming lost. Rough dirt roads leading to the trailhead may be impassable in wet weather. A four-wheel drive vehicle is recommended in the winter and spring and may be needed at other times. Deeply rutted sections require high clearance. Check with backcountry rangers for current road conditions. There may be a fee collected for crossing the Havasupai Indian Reservation.

Route
Leaving the rim, the trail angles through the Kaibab and Toroweap Formations as it descends to the bed of a drainage coming from the east. The route crosses the wash and contours above the Coconino Sandstone past an old wire fence to a break leading below. Steep switchbacks descend the Coconino cliffs to a broad terrace called the Esplanade.

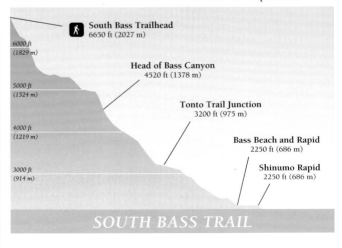

South Bass Trailhead
6650 ft (2027 m)

6000 ft
(1829 m)

Head of Bass Canyon
4520 ft (1378 m)

5000 ft
(1524 m)

Tonto Trail Junction
3200 ft (975 m)

4000 ft
(1219 m)

Bass Beach and Rapid
2250 ft (686 m)

3000 ft
(914 m)

Shinumo Rapid
2250 ft (686 m)

SOUTH BASS TRAIL

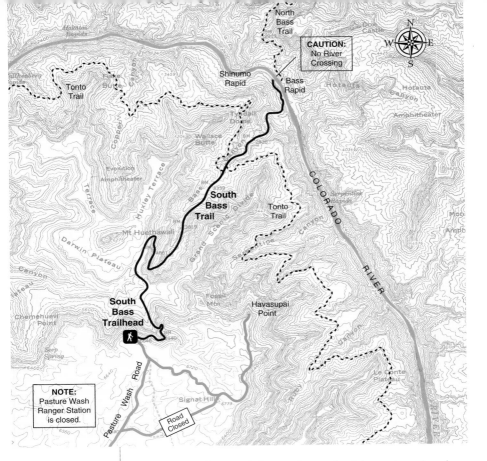

family's dirty clothes and saddle her horse for a three-day trip to the river and back.

In 1915, a river party abandoned their metal boat, the Ross Wheeler, that still lies at the foot of the Bass Trail.

A generally level footpath marked by cairns heads northwest across the Esplanade. Skirting the east side of Mt. Huethawali, the trail reaches a break in the Supai Group. Dropping below the Esplanade, the trail rounds a promontory and begins a descending traverse to the south. This leads to a distinct break in the Redwall cliff at the head of Bass Canyon.

The route turns north and descends through the Redwall Limestone. After crossing the brushy wash several times, the trail leaves the drainage and stays high on the east side of Bass Canyon. Eventually the trail drops back to the creek bed where it remains until near the river. Seasonal water may sometimes be found in a deep bedrock pothole where the trail detours around a pouroff. Approaching the river, the route leaves the drainage and heads west a short distance where a cairn marks a rough spur trail leading to a beach above Bass Rapid. The mapped trail continues farther west to the site of an old cable crossing and an overlook of Shinumo Rapid.

BOUCHER TRAIL

Length
- 10.5 miles (16.9 km): Hermit trailhead to Boucher Rapid
- 9.5 miles (15.3 km): Dripping Springs Trail junction to Boucher Rapid
- 8 miles (12.9 km): Boucher trailhead to Boucher Rapid

Maps:

*Bright Angel
(15 minute)*

*Grand Canyon
(7.5 minute)*

Elevations
- 5280 feet (1609 m): Boucher trailhead at junction with Dripping Springs Trail
- 2760 feet (841 m): Boucher Creek

Water Sources
- Dripping Springs
- Boucher Creek
- Colorado River

*Part-time hermit
Louis Boucher
first came to the
canyon in 1891
and soon began
guiding tourists and
prospecting for
mineral deposits.*

*He built a camp
at Dripping Springs
and a cabin near
his copper mine in
Boucher Canyon
where he planted an*

Trail Conditions
Wilderness Trail. Steep sections with numerous washouts require some route finding. Very strenuous hike.

Trailhead
To reach the Boucher Trail, take the upper Hermit Trail to the Dripping Springs Trail in Hermit Basin (also known as Waldron Basin). Follow it west about 1 mile (1.6 km) until reaching the signed trailhead at a drainage coming from the west.

An alternate approach begins at the Dripping Springs trailhead on the rim south of Eremita Mesa. The road to it is closed to vehicles. Park along Boundary Road and walk to trailhead. Check with backcountry rangers for current conditions and closure information.

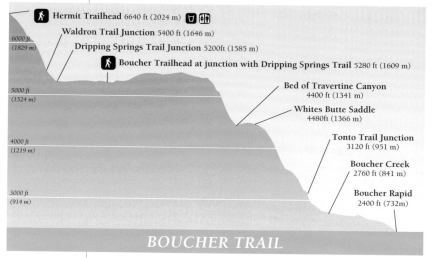

Hermit Trailhead 6640 ft (2024 m)

Waldron Trail Junction 5400 ft (1646 m)

Dripping Springs Trail Junction 5200ft (1585 m)

Boucher Trailhead at junction with Dripping Springs Trail 5280 ft (1609 m)

6000 ft (1829 m)

5000 ft (1524 m)

4000 ft (1219 m)

3000 ft (914 m)

Bed of Travertine Canyon 4400 ft (1341 m)

Whites Butte Saddle 4480ft (1366 m)

Tonto Trail Junction 3120 ft (951 m)

Boucher Creek 2760 ft (841 m)

Boucher Rapid 2400 ft (732m)

BOUCHER TRAIL

24

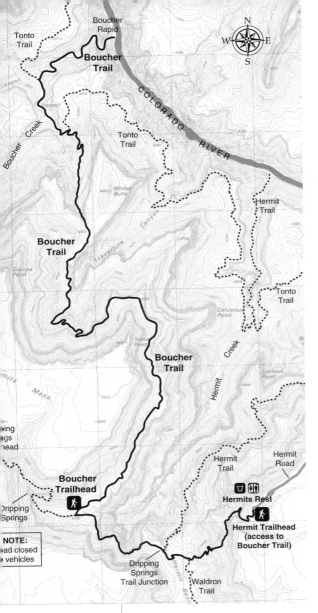

From the Dripping Springs trailhead, descend to the drainage and cross to the north side where the trail switchbacks through the Coconino Sandstone. At its base a rock basin catches spring water dripping from clumps of maidenhair fern hanging from an overhanging cliff. Continue past the springs for 0.75 miles (1.2 km) until reaching the Boucher Trail sign.

Route

Boucher Trail contours along a shelf at the top of the Supai Group for the first 3 miles (4.8 km). It rounds Yuma Point before reaching the descent route through the Supai. Several very steep, exposed sections require hand-and-foot scrambling through the Supai cliffs. Pay attention to the line of descent the trail takes to the bed of Travertine Canyon.

Once below the Supai Group, stay on the west side of Travertine Canyon until reaching the saddle south of Whites Butte. The trail descends abruptly through the Redwall, Temple Butte, and Muav cliffs on the northwest side of the saddle. Be careful of loose rock and steep grades. The route runs north to join the Tonto Trail. Veering off the Tonto, the trail intersects Boucher Creek. It continues down the creek bed another 1.5 miles (2.4 km) along a boulder-hopping route to the Colorado River.

orchard of 75 fruit trees. Remains of the cabin are still visible on the east side of Boucher Creek.

WALDRON TRAIL

Maps:

*Bright Angel
(15 minute)*

*Grand Canyon
(7.5 minute)*

Length
• 2 miles (3.2 km): Waldron trailhead (Horsethief Tank) to Hermit Trail

Elevation
• 6420 feet (1957 m): Waldron trailhead (Horsethief Tank)
• 5400 feet (1646 m): Hermit Trail junction

Water Source
• No water

Trail Conditions
Wilderness Trail. Occasional washouts require some route-finding skill.

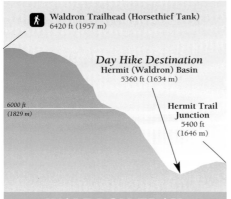

Waldron Trailhead (Horsethief Tank)
6420 ft (1957 m)

Day Hike Destination
Hermit (Waldron) Basin
5360 ft (1634 m)

6000 ft
(1829 m)

**Hermit Trail
Junction**
5400 ft
(1646 m)

WALDRON TRAIL

Trailhead
Waldron trailhead is located 6 miles southwest of Grand Canyon Village. Access is via Rowe Well Road and various connecting (unnamed) dirt roads. Four-wheel drive is recommended; roads are impassable in winter. Road closures may prevent direct access to Horsethief Tank.

Route
From the trailhead at Horsethief Tank the trail descends through a talus-covered section of Coconino Sandstone into Hermit (Waldron) Basin. Because of its heavy pinyon-juniper cover, this trail stays cooler in the summer than the Hermit Trail, but views of the main canyon are more limited. Hermit Basin and the rim above are good areas to see wildlife, especially mule deer, and they make excellent day-hike destinations.

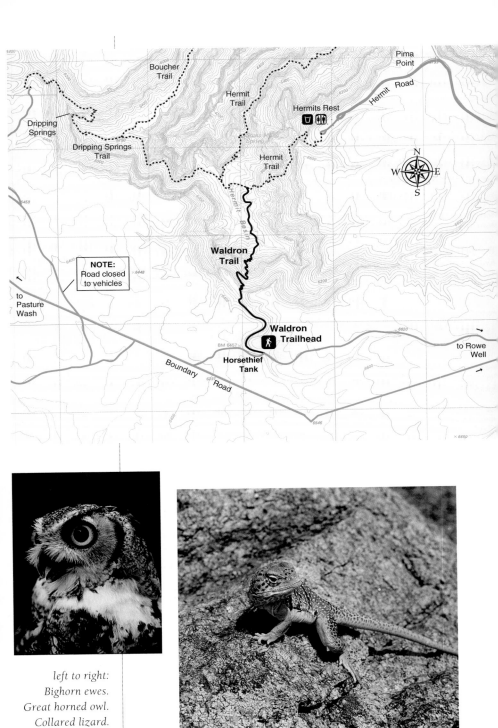

Boucher
Trail

Hermit
Trail

Pima
Point

Hermit Road

Hermits Rest

Dripping
Springs

Dripping Springs
Trail

Hermit
Trail

Hermit Basin

**Waldron
Trail**

NOTE:
Road closed
to vehicles

to
Pasture
Wash

BM 6457

**Waldron
Trailhead**

to Rowe
Well

Boundary Road

**Horsethief
Tank**

*left to right:
Bighorn ewes.
Great horned owl.
Collared lizard.*

27

HERMIT TRAIL

Length
- 2.5 miles (4.0 km): Hermit trailhead to Santa Maria Springs
- 7.8 miles (12.6 km): Hermit trailhead to Hermit Creek
- 9.3 miles (15.0 km): Hermit trailhead to Colorado River

Maps:

Bright Angel (15 minute)

Grand Canyon (7.5 minute)

Elevations
- 6640 feet (2024 m): Hermit trailhead
- 4880 feet (1487 m): Santa Maria Springs
- 2400 feet (732 m): Colorado River

Water Sources
- Santa Maria Springs
- Hermit Creek
- Colorado River

The Santa Fe Railroad began developing the Hermit Canyon area so that travelers could avoid paying tolls on the Bright Angel Trail. A tramway from Pima Point supplied the tourist camp in Hermit Canyon.

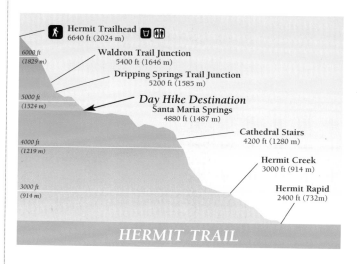

Hermit Trailhead
6640 ft (2024 m)

6000 ft (1829 m)

Waldron Trail Junction
5400 ft (1646 m)

Dripping Springs Trail Junction
5200 ft (1585 m)

5000 ft (1524 m)

Day Hike Destination
Santa Maria Springs
4880 ft (1487 m)

Cathedral Stairs
4200 ft (1280 m)

4000 ft (1219 m)

Hermit Creek
3000 ft (914 m)

3000 ft (914 m)

Hermit Rapid
2400 ft (732m)

HERMIT TRAIL

NOTE: Overnight hikers must camp in designated campsites at Hermit Creek and Hermit Rapid.

***Allow 7 hours** to reach Hermit Creek. The trail is rocky and steep, and requires very slow walking.*

Trail Conditions
Wilderness Trail. Occasional washouts require some route-finding skill.

Trailhead
Hermit Trail begins at the end of the service road behind Hermits Rest, located at the end of Hermit Road, 8 miles (12.8 km) west of Grand Canyon Village. Use the free shuttle to access the trailhead.

Route
The trail switchbacks into Hermit Canyon and swings north to the head of Hermit Gorge. Dropping into the gorge, it follows a series of long traverses and short descents through the Supai cliffs. Rock slides obscure portions of the trail. The route leaves this slide area where it meets the Redwall Formation.

The Redwall descent follows a series of tight switchbacks known as the Cathedral Stairs. Angling across a talus slope below Cope Butte, the Hermit Trail intersects the Tonto Trail and heads left (west) toward Hermit Creek. The trail follows the creek 1.5 miles (2.4 km) to the Colorado River and a view of the high standing waves of Hermit Rapid.

Variations

Waldron Trail, 2 miles (3.2 km) long, begins on the rim at the head of Hermit Canyon near Horsethief Tank. Switch-backing below the rim, it crosses Hermit Basin and joins the Hermit Trail.

Dripping Springs Trail, branches off Hermit Trail at the head of Hermit Gorge. Distance to Dripping Springs from Hermit trailhead is 3 miles (4.8 km) one way. Water is available at Dripping Springs but must be treated. The Dripping Springs Trail continues past the springs and climbs to the rim.

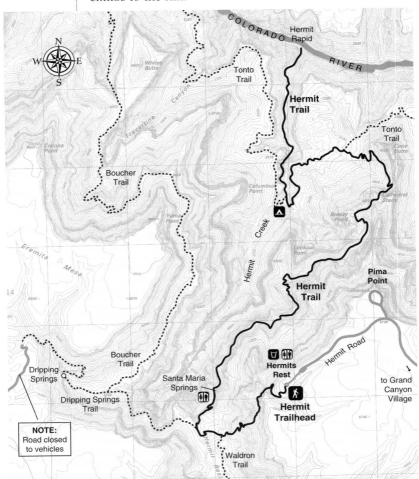

BRIGHT ANGEL TRAIL

Maps:

Bright Angel
(15 minute)

Grand Canyon
Phantom Ranch
(7.5 minute)

Since prehistoric
times, Indians used
the natural route
along the fault line to
enter the inner canyon
and reach the springs
at Indian Garden.
Indian pictographs
may be seen above

Length
- 4.6 miles (7.4 km): Bright Angel trailhead to Indian Garden
- 6.1 miles (9.8 km): Bright Angel trailhead to Plateau Point
- 7.8 miles (12.6 km): Bright Angel trailhead to the Colorado River
- 9.3 miles (15 km): Bright Angel trailhead to Bright Angel Campground

Elevations
- 6860 feet (2091 m): Bright Angel trailhead
- 3800 feet (1158 m): Indian Garden
- 3740 feet (1140 m): Plateau Point
- 2480 feet (756 m): Colorado River

Water Sources
- Mile-and-a-Half Resthouse and Three-Mile Resthouse (May through September)
- Indian Garden
- Colorado River
- Bright Angel Campground

Trail Conditions
Corridor Trail. Well maintained and well marked.

Trailhead
Bright Angel Trail begins next to Kolb Studio in Grand Canyon Village. (See map on pages 32-33.)

Bright Angel Trailhead
6860 ft (2091 m)

6000 ft
(1829 m)

Mile-and-a-Half Resthouse
5720 ft (1743 m)

Three-Mile Resthouse
4920 ft (1500 m)

5000 ft
(1524 m)

Maximum
Day Hike Destination
Plateau Point/Tonto Trail Junction
3760 ft (1146 m)

Indian Garden
3800 ft (1158 m)

4000 ft
(1219 m)

Bright Angel Campground

River Resthouse
2480 ft (756 m)

Phantom Ranch

Bright Angel Suspension Bridge

3000 ft
(914 m)

BRIGHT ANGEL TRAIL

*Bright Angel Trail,
South Rim.*

*the trail just past
the first tunnel and
above the trail
between Mile-and-a-
Half Resthouse and
Two-Mile Corner.*

*Miners improved the
trail in 1891 and
began charging a toll
for others to use it.*

*Private citizens, the
Santa Fe Railway,
and government
officials contested
ownership of the
Bright Angel Trail
from 1901 to 1928,
when control finally
passed to the National
Park Service.*

*Havasupai families
still farmed at Indian
Garden around the
turn of the century.*

*NOTE:
Mule riders take day
trips down the trail to
Plateau Point and
overnight trips to
Phantom Ranch.*

*When a mule party
approaches, stand
quietly to the inside of
the trail until it has
passed. Mules have
the right of way.*

Route

The trail descends through a natural break in the upper
cliffs, passing the Redwall Limestone in a series of tight
switchbacks called Jacobs Ladder. The trail follows Garden
Creek below Indian Garden, threading the Tapeats narrows.
Leaving the creek, the trail descends through the Vishnu
Schist in a series of switchbacks called the Devils
Corkscrew. It joins the River Trail, branching right (east),
just before reaching the Colorado River. The trail continues
1.5 miles (2.4 km) along the river to the Bright Angel
Suspension Bridge, which leads to Bright Angel Camp-
ground and Phantom Ranch on the north side of the river.

*Emergency phones are located at Mile-and-a-Half Rest-
house, Three-Mile Resthouse, and the River Resthouse, as well as
at Indian Garden and Bright Angel Campground.*

Variation

Plateau Point Trail leads 1.5 miles (2.4 km) from Indian
Garden to a dramatic view of the Inner Gorge and the river
1300 feet (396 m) below.

31

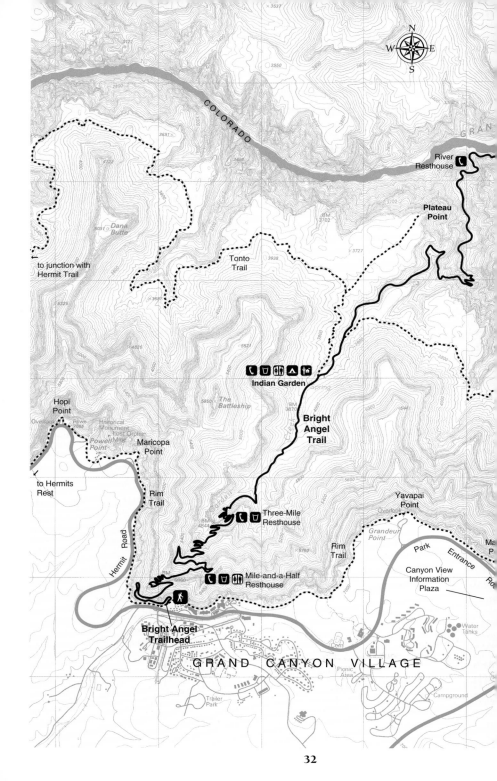

N
W E
S

COLORADO

GRAN

× 3537

3950

3691 ×

Dana
Butte

to junction with
Hermit Trail

Tonto
Trail

3938

River
Resthouse

BM
3702

Plateau
Point

3727

Indian Garden

Spring

The
Battleship

BM
387

Bright
Angel
Trail

Hopi
Point

Historical
Monument

Maricopa
Point

Powell
Point

to Hermits
Rest

Rim
Trail

Hermit   Road

Three-Mile
Resthouse

BM
4844

Yavapai
Point

Grandeur
Point

Rim
Trail

Mile-and-a-Half
Resthouse

BM

Park   Entrance   Ro

Ma
P

Canyon View
Information
Plaza

Bright Angel
Trailhead

GRAND   CANYON   VILLAGE

Cem

Picnic
Area

Water
Tanks

Trailer
Park

Campground

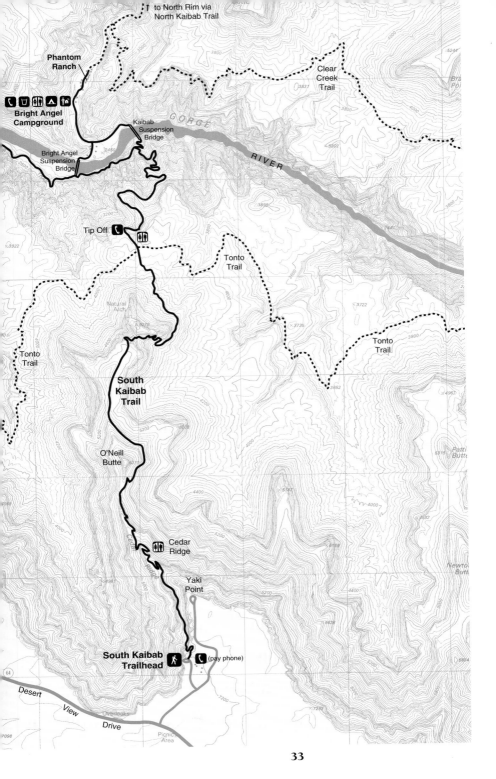

to North Rim via
North Kaibab Trail

Phantom
Ranch

Clear
Creek
Trail

Bright Angel
Campground

Kaibab
Suspension
Bridge

GORGE

Bright Angel
Suspension
Bridge

RIVER

Tip Off

Tonto
Trail

Tonto
Trail

Tonto
Trail

Natural
Arch

South
Kaibab
Trail

O'Neill
Butte

Cedar
Ridge

Yaki
Point

South Kaibab
Trailhead

(pay phone)

Desert

View

Drive

Overlooks

Picnic
Area

33

SOUTH KAIBAB TRAIL

Length
- 1.5 miles (2.4 km): South Kaibab trailhead to Cedar Ridge
- 6.3 miles (10.1 km): South Kaibab trailhead to the Colorado River
- 7.3 miles (11.7 km): South Kaibab trailhead to Bright Angel Campground

Maps:

Bright Angel (15 minute)

Phantom Ranch (7.5 minute)

Elevations
- 7260 feet (2213 m): South Kaibab trailhead
- 6320 feet (1926 m): Cedar Ridge
- 2480 feet (756 m): Colorado River

Water Sources
- Colorado River
- Bright Angel Campground

Trail Conditions
Corridor Trail. Well maintained and well marked.

The National Park Service completed the cross-canyon "corridor" trail system in 1928— the same year it took control of the Bright Angel Trail.

Most trails in the Grand Canyon stay within the confines of a side canyon. But the South Kaibab is one of the few trails to follow open ridgelines that provide panoramic views of the main gorge.

Trailhead
Take the Yaki Point turnoff on Desert View Drive and then turn onto the first paved road to the left (west). The South Kaibab trailhead is well marked, lying just north of the parking area at the end of the road. (See map on pages 32-33.) Use the free shuttle bus to access the trailhead.

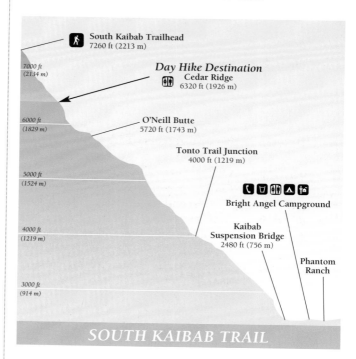

South Kaibab Trailhead
7260 ft (2213 m)

7000 ft (2134 m)

Day Hike Destination
Cedar Ridge
6320 ft (1926 m)

6000 ft (1829 m)

O'Neill Butte
5720 ft (1743 m)

Tonto Trail Junction
4000 ft (1219 m)

5000 ft (1524 m)

Bright Angel Campground

4000 ft (1219 m)

Kaibab
Suspension Bridge
2480 ft (756 m)

Phantom Ranch

3000 ft (914 m)

SOUTH KAIBAB TRAIL

South Kaibab Trail, South Rim.

Route

The trail zigzags quickly through the upper cliffs before traversing north. After descending another series of switchbacks, it reaches Cedar Ridge, 1.5 miles (2.4 km) from the rim. The walk to Cedar Ridge and back to the rim is one of the park's most popular day hikes. A toilet is available at Cedar Ridge, but no water.

Descending the east side of Cedar Ridge in a long traverse, the trail continues north past O'Neill Butte until reaching a long series of switchbacks through the Redwall Limestone. The trail angles steeply down to the Tonto Platform. The descent into the Inner Gorge begins at the Tipoff shortly after the trail intersects the Tonto Trail. An emergency telephone and toilet are located at the Tipoff.

Reaching the bottom of the gorge, the trail crosses the Colorado River on the Kaibab Suspension Bridge and continues to the Bright Angel Campground.

NOTE:
Because the South Kaibab Trail is steep and without water between the river and the rim, park rangers do not recommend ascending it during the summer months.

GRANDVIEW TRAIL

Length
- 3 miles (4.8 km): Grandview trailhead to Horseshoe Mesa
- 4.8 miles (7.7 km): Grandview trailhead to Tonto Trail junction via East Horseshoe Mesa Trail

Elevations
- 7400 feet (2256 m): Grandview trailhead
- 4800 feet (1463 m): Horseshoe Mesa
- 3760 feet (1146 m): Tonto Trail junction

Water Source
- Water is not available along the trail or on Horseshoe Mesa. The nearest water source is Page (Miners) Spring at the bottom of the Redwall, 400 feet (122 m) below the east rim of Horseshoe Mesa.

Trail Conditions
Wilderness Trail. Some washouts, but route finding is not difficult. In winter, upper portions of trail may be dangerous due to packed snow and ice. Use instep crampons in winter.

Trailhead
Grandview Trail begins at the parking area on Grandview Point, off Desert View Drive between Grand Canyon Village and Desert View.

Maps:

Vishnu Temple
Grandview Point
(15 minute)

Grandview Point
Cape Royal
(7.5 minute)

Hopi Indians gathered mineral paints on Horseshoe Mesa long before Pete Berry began working the Last Chance Mine in 1890.

Berry built a trail to his copper mine and used burros to pack the ore to the rim. The copper tested high grade, but transportation costs cut into his profits.

When tourism increased, Berry built the Grandview Hotel on the rim and began guiding sightseers into the canyon along his trail.

All mining ended on the mesa in 1908.

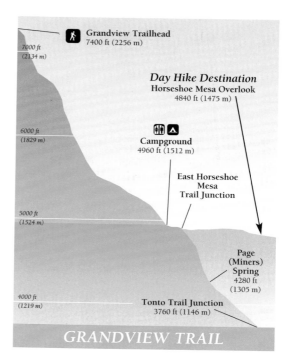

Grandview Trailhead
7400 ft (2256 m)

7000 ft
(2134 m)

Day Hike Destination
Horseshoe Mesa Overlook
4840 ft (1475 m)

6000 ft
(1829 m)

Campground
4960 ft (1512 m)

East Horseshoe
Mesa
Trail Junction

5000 ft
(1524 m)

Page
(Miners)
Spring
4280 ft
(1305 m)

4000 ft
(1219 m)

Tonto Trail Junction
3760 ft (1146 m)

GRANDVIEW TRAIL

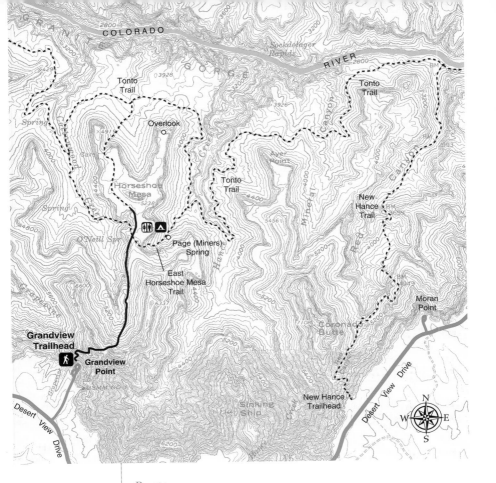

Route

Descending the north end of Grandview Point, the trail crosses a narrow saddle between upper Hance and Grapevine Canyons. It rounds a point and continues its descent, switchbacking through the Coconino Sandstone. After dropping steeply through the Hermit Shale and into the Supai Group, the trail gradually angles downward to Horseshoe Mesa above the Redwall Limestone.

Variation

East Horseshoe Mesa Trail follows a break on the east side of the narrow neck leading to the mesa. Rockslides and washouts in the Redwall have eroded portions of it. After passing a spur trail to Page (Miners) Spring, the footpath continues to the Tonto Trail. Other routes, descending the west side of the mesa and its northwest arm, connect Horseshoe Mesa with the Tonto Trail.

Warning:
Do not enter the mine shafts. Most are unstable and some contain vertical shafts. Radon levels in the mines register many times above normal levels.

Prehistoric and historic artifacts found within the park are protected by law. Leave them for others to enjoy.

NEW HANCE TRAIL
(RED CANYON TRAIL)

Maps:

Grandview Point
Vishnu Temple
(15 minute)

Grandview Point
Cape Royal
(7.5 minute)

An outcropping of Precambrian schist near Hance Rapid marks the beginning of Granite Gorge, an area of concern to early river runners because of dangerous rapids and difficult portages. Hakatai Shale forms the distinctive red rock along the lower stretch of Red Canyon. The east end of the Tonto Trail begins at the mouth of Red Canyon.

John Hance, famous canyon guide and storyteller, arrived at the South Rim about 1883. Hance first built a trail down Hance Creek to the west, following a

Length
- 8 miles (12.9 km): New Hance trailhead to the Colorado River

Elevations
- 7000 feet (2134 m): New Hance trailhead
- 2600 feet (792 m): Colorado River

Water Source
- Colorado River

Trail Conditions
Wilderness Trail. Washouts and rockslides require some route-finding ability.

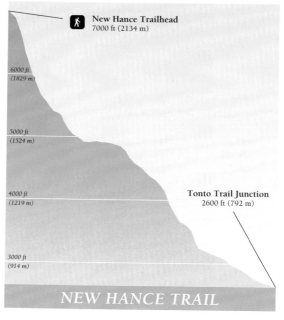

New Hance Trailhead
7000 ft (2134 m)

6000 ft
(1829 m)

5000 ft
(1524 m)

4000 ft
(1219 m)

Tonto Trail Junction
2600 ft (792 m)

3000 ft
(914 m)

NEW HANCE TRAIL

Trailhead
Park at Moran Point and walk about 1 mile (1.6 km) south along the rim to a trail sign.

Route
The trail switchbacks downward, past occasional washouts, to the base of the Coconino Sandstone. Crosstrails sometimes make the main trail difficult to follow. The trail continues to the head of a major drainage on the east side of the Coronado Butte saddle.

The route follows this drainage, descending to the top of the Redwall cliff. Continuing along the rim on the east

38

ohn Hance, late 1800s.

Havasupai Indian
*oute. When his orig-
nal trail washed out,
he relocated it to its
present location in
Red Canyon.*

*"You must under-
stand," Hance once
warned a tourist,
"that when you get
to the bottom of the
canyon and reach
the shore of the
Colorado River it
is very warm. You
can't imagine how
hot it is. Why, I'll
give my word, I've
been down there
when it was so
hot it melted the
wings off the flies."*

*"But," asked an
incredulous lady
from New England,
"how do the tourists
stand it?"*

*"Madame," Hance
replied, "I have
never yet seen a
tourist with wings!"*

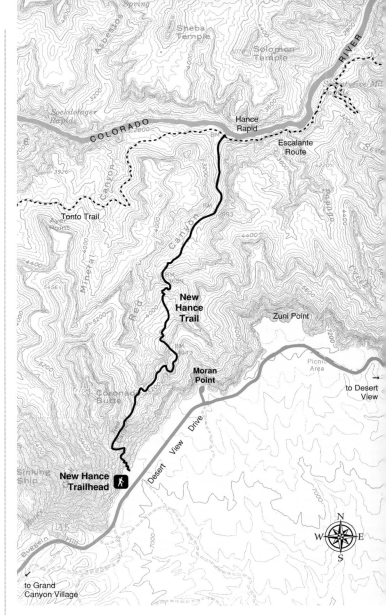

side, it passes several drainages before reaching the Redwall
break. The descent route is marked by a large cairn.

Once through the Redwall cliff, the route descends
a long talus slope and crosses a major drainage before
reaching the bed of Red Canyon. Seasonal water may be
found upstream. The trail follows the creekbed downstream
to the river.

TANNER TRAIL

Maps:

Vishnu Temple (15 minute)

Desert View (7.5 minute)

Seth Tanner, an early Mormon pioneer, improved this prehistoric Indian footpath in the 1880s. His pack trail provided access to mining claims along the river in the Palisades Creek area.

At one time the route was part of the Horsethief Trail. Outlaws stole horses in Utah and drove them down the Nankoweap Trail to a low-water ford across the Colorado River. After altering brands, they moved the horses up the Tanner Trail to the South Rim and sold them farther south to unsuspecting ranchers.

Length
• 3 miles (4.8 km): Tanner trailhead to Escalante Butte
• about 10 miles (16.1 km): Tanner trailhead to the Colorado River

Elevations
• 7300 feet (2225 m): Tanner trailhead
• 5600 feet (1707 m): Escalante Saddle
• 2700 feet (823 m): Colorado River

Water Source
• Colorado River

Trail Conditions
Wilderness Trail. Washouts and rockslides require some route-finding skill. Hot and dry in summer. Stash water on way in for use on way out. Use instep crampons in winter.

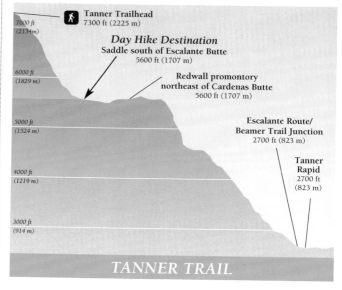

Trailhead
Tanner Trail begins just east of the Lipan Point parking area.

Route
The trail follows a series of switchbacks down steep talus slopes at the head of the west branch of Tanner Canyon. It stays on the west side of the drainage as it drops through the Hermit and most of the Supai Group.

The route leaves the drainage and contours around the base of Escalante and Cardenas Buttes on a broad bench for about 3 miles (4.8 km). Reaching a break in the Redwall

40

cliff, it descends steeply toward the bed of Tanner Canyon and then veers northward. The trail stays high as it gradually descends along the west side of Tanner Canyon, entering the bed of the drainage near the Colorado River.

Variations

Beamer Trail: About 9.5 miles (15.3 km) from Tanner Beach to mouth of Little Colorado River (LCR). Generally the route follows near the river as far as Palisade Creek, then climbs via cairned switchbacks to the top of the Tapeats Sandstone and follows this narrow bench to the LCR. No camping is allowed within 0.25 mile of the LCR/Colorado River junction.

Escalante Route: About 15 miles (24 km) from Tanner Trail to New Hance Trail. This rugged route presents difficulties not normally encountered along the Tonto Trail. Several sections require exposed hand-and-toe climbing and vertical pack handling. No water except at the river. For experienced Grand Canyon hikers only.

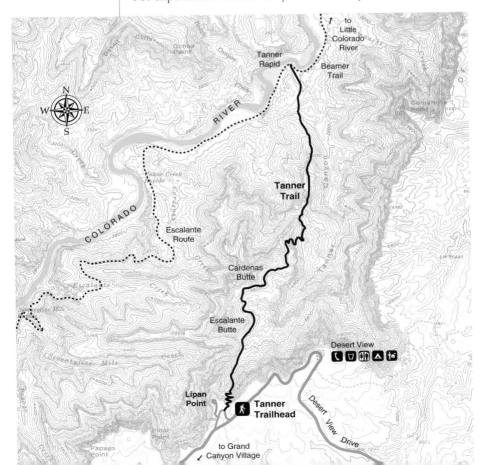

TONTO TRAIL

Maps:

Vishnu Temple
Bright Angel
Havasupai Point
(15 minute)

Cape Royal
Phantom Ranch
Grand Canyon
Shiva Temple
Piute Point
Havasupai Point
Explorers Monument
(7.5 minute)

Length

• 95 miles (152.9 km): Garnet Canyon to Red Canyon

Hikers seldom follow the entire Tonto Trail, normally using it to connect with rim-to-river routes. Approximate mileages between key points on the Tonto Trail:

• 11.6 miles (18.7 km): Garnet Creek to Bass Canyon
• 35.7 miles (57.5 km): Bass Canyon to Hermit Creek
• 12 miles (19.3 km): Hermit Creek to Bright Angel Trail (Indian Garden)
• 4.5 miles (7.2 km): Bright Angel Trail to South Kaibab Trail
• 21.3 miles (34.3 km): South Kaibab Trail to Grandview Trail (Horseshoe Mesa)
• 9.9 miles (15.9 km): Grandview Trail to New Hance Trail (Red Canyon)

Elevations

• 3600 feet (1097 m): Tonto Platform (Red Canyon)
• 2800 feet (853 m): Tonto Platform (Garnet Canyon)

NOTE:
To eliminate the buildup of human waste along heavily-traveled sections of the Tonto Trail, toilets are located at the Tipoff and at Horn, Salt, Monument, and Hermit Creeks. Please use them.

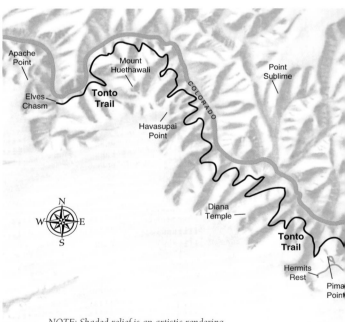

NOTE: Shaded relief is an artistic rendering and is not accurate in detail. Simplified trail is shown for orientation purposes only, and is not intended for route finding in the field.

Water Sources
- Boucher, Hermit, Monument, Pipe, Hance, and Grapevine Creeks
- Indian Garden
- Seasonal water may be found at Garnet, Ruby, Turquoise, Slate, Salt, and Cottonwood Creeks.
- Access to the Colorado River at the foot of Bass, Monument, and Serpentine Canyons, and at the mouth of Red Canyon.

Trail Conditions
Wilderness Trail. Washouts and intersecting game trails require route finding. West of Slate Canyon, the Tonto Trail becomes less distinct.

Route
Tonto Trail follows the Tonto Platform for its entire length. Winding in and out of drainages, the route is not as level as it appears from the rim and is hard to follow in places. When approaching major drainages, spot where the trail continues on the far side of the drainage before descending.

Thunder
River

Bill Hall

Great Thumb

Mesa

North Bass

KAIBAB

NATIONAL

FOREST

G R A N D   C A N Y O N

COLORADO

Point
Sublime

HAVASUPAI

INDIAN

RESERVATION

Pima
Point

Hermit Road

Hermits
Rest

NOTE: Shaded relief is an artistic rendering
and is not accurate in detail. Simplified trails
are shown for orientation purposes only, and
are not intended for route finding in the field.

NORTH RIM TRAILS

↑ to Jacob Lake and Kanab

↑ to Lees Ferry

oab dge

De Motte

67

Road closed in winter.

Park Entrance

N A V A J O

I N D I A N

R E S E R V A T I O N

Nankoweap

Point Imperial

N A T I O N A L   P A R K

Vista Encantadora

Ken Patrick

Uncle Jim

Widforss

North Kaibab

Transept

Grand Canyon Lodge

Bright Angel Point

Little Colorado River

Walhalla Overlook

Cliff Springs

Cape Royal

Phantom Ranch

Clear Creek

Cape Royal

Bright Angel

South Kaibab

Canyon View Information Plaza

R I V E R

Desert View

Grand Canyon Village

Desert

View

Drive

Tusayan Ruins

Tusayan

Park Entrance

64

64

to Williams and Flagstaff

K A I B A B   N A T I O N A L   F O R E S T

to Cameron ↘

NORTH RIM TRAILS

HIKING ALONG THE RIM

TRAILS WIND ALONG the brink of the Grand Canyon through mixed-conifer forests where an observant hiker will encounter an interesting diversity of plant and animal life. These pathways lead to panoramic views of the inner canyon and distant views of the Painted Desert to the east or the South Rim which lies an average of 1000 feet (305 m) lower than the North Rim. These rim trails offer less strenuous hiking, cooler temperatures, and more shade than the inner canyon trail system.

Uncle Jim Owens, 1926.

Uncle Jim Owens guided celebrities such as western novelist Zane Grey and former president Teddy Roosevelt on mountain lion hunts.

It was originally believed that killing mountain lions would improve the deer herds, but without predators the deer population exploded, causing overgrazing and massive starvation.

Today, mountain lions and all other wildlife within the park are protected by law.

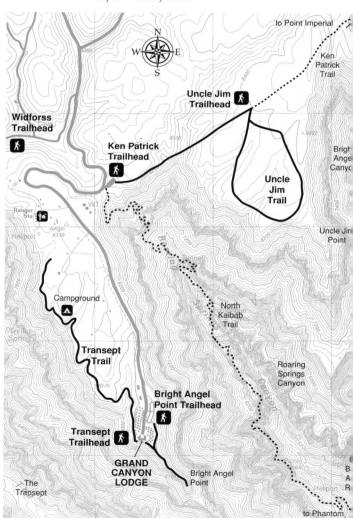

SHORTER TRAILS

Geologist Clarence Dutton named The Transept in 1882 and considered it "far grander than Yosemite."

Bright Angel Point Trail: 0.5 mile (0.8 km)
The paved trail runs from the Grand Canyon Lodge parking lot along a knife-edge ridge separating Roaring Springs Canyon and The Transept. A self-guiding trail brochure is available at the log shelter adjacent to the parking lot or at the lodge.

Transept Trail: 1.5 miles (2.4 km)
Skirting the canyon rim, the trail leads from Bright Angel Lodge to the campground. The well-marked route overlooks a side canyon called The Transept.

Cliff Springs Trail: 1 mile (1.6 km)
The trail begins across the road from Angels Window Overlook and descends a ravine past a small prehistoric ruin to the cliff-sheltered spring. (See map, page 45.)

Cape Royal Trail: 0.6 miles (1 km)
The paved trail leaves the parking area at the end of the road and winds past Angels Window to the tip of Walhalla Plateau. (See map, page 45.)

UNCLE JIM TRAIL

Maps:

Bright Angel (15 minute)

Bright Angel Point (7.5 minute)

During his dozen years as game warden on the North Rim, Uncle Jim Owens claimed to have shot more than 500 mountain lions.

Length
• 2.5 miles (4 km): Ken Patrick trailhead to Uncle Jim Point. Round-trip is 5 miles (8 km).

Elevations
• 8300 feet (2530 m): Ken Patrick trailhead
• 8244 feet (2513 m): Uncle Jim Point

Water Source
• No water

Trail Conditions
Well marked with gentle gradients.

Trailhead
Uncle Jim Trail begins at the Ken Patrick trailhead on the east side of the parking area for the North Kaibab Trail, 2 miles (3.2 km) north of the Grand Canyon Lodge.

Route
The trail skirts the head of Roaring Springs Canyon, then winds south through the forest to a viewpoint near Uncle Jim Point that overlooks the upper sections of the North Kaibab Trail. The trail loops along the rim of Bright Angel Canyon.

WIDFORSS TRAIL

Length
- 5 miles (8 km): Widforss trailhead to Widforss Point. Round-trip is 10 miles (16 km).

Elevations
- 8100 feet (2469 m): Widforss trailhead
- 7900 feet (2408 m): Widforss Point

Maps:

*Bright Angel
(15 minute)*

*Bright Angel Point
(7.5 minute)*

Water Source
- No water

Trail Conditions
Well-marked trail with mild gradients.

Trailhead
Take the gravel road that begins across from the North Kaibab Trail parking area, 2 miles (3.2 km) north of the Grand Canyon Lodge. The Widforss Trail parking area is located 0.25 mile (0.4 km) from the paved road. Park rangers have designed the first 2.5 miles (4 km) as a self-guided nature trail. Pick up an interpretive brochure at the trailhead.

Route
Widforss Trail follows the canyon rim as it skirts The Transept, a large tributary gorge of Bright Angel Canyon. The trail winds through a mixed spruce-fir forest to a picnic area near Widforss Point overlooking Haunted Canyon.

Widforss Point honors artist Gunnar M. Widforss who painted landscapes in the national parks of the West during the 1920s and 1930s.

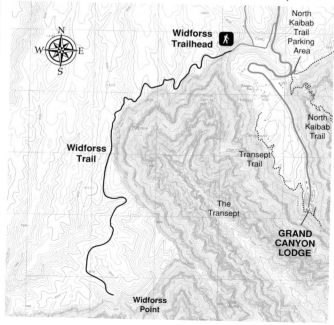

KEN PATRICK TRAIL

Maps:

*Bright Angel
DeMotte Park
Nankoweap
(15 minute)*

*Bright Angel Point
Point Imperial
(7.5 minute)*

*Once called Skiddoo
Point, Point Imperial
is the highest view-
point on either rim.*

Length
- 10 miles (16.1 km): Ken Patrick trailhead to Point Imperial

Elevations
- 8250 feet (2515 m): Ken Patrick trailhead
- 8803 feet (2683 m): Point Imperial

Water Source
- No water

Trail Conditions
Some portions are well marked, others are obscure.

Trailhead
Ken Patrick Trail begins on the east side of the North Kaibab trailhead parking lot.

Route
The trail skirts the rim in several locations and winds through the forest, becoming difficult to follow once past the Old Bright Angel trailhead. The trail crosses numerous drainages and often detours around fallen trees. After intersecting the Cape Royal Road, the trail again becomes more distinct as it continues to Point Imperial.

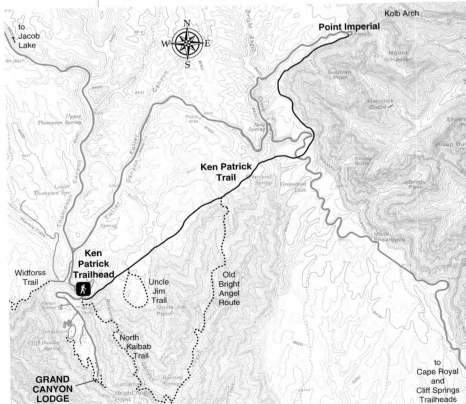

THUNDER RIVER TRAIL

Maps:

*Powell Plateau
(15 minute)*

*Tapeats Amphitheater
Fishtail Mesa
Powell Plateau
(7.5 minute)*

*Rumors of placer gold
drew miners into the
area in 1876. They
constructed the upper
portions of the trail,
used by geologist
Clarence Dutton
several years later.*

*Crews built the present
trail into Tapeats
Creek in 1926.*

*Thunder River, one of
the world's shortest
rivers, flows for only
0.5 mile (0.8 km)
before entering
Tapeats Creek.*

Length
- about 15 miles (24 km): Thunder River trailhead (Indian Hollow) to the Colorado River
- about 12 miles (19.3 km): Bill Hall trailhead (Monument Point) to the Colorado River

Elevations
- 6400 feet (1950 m): Thunder River trailhead
- 7200 feet (2194 m): Bill Hall trailhead
- 2000 feet (609 m): Colorado River

Water Sources
- Thunder River
- Tapeats Creek
- Colorado River
- Deer Creek can be accessed from Surprise Valley

Trail Conditions
Wilderness Trail. Occasional washouts require some route-finding ability. Extremely hot and dry in summer. Stash water (1 gal/4.5 l) on your way in for use on the way out.

Bill Hall Trailhead
Monument Point 7200 ft (2195 m)

7000 ft (2134 m)

Thunder River Trailhead
Indian Hollow 6400 ft (1951 m)

6000 ft (1829 m)

Thunder River Trail
Thunder Spring Cave
3400 ft (1036 m)

Junction
5640 ft (1719 m)

5000 ft (1524 m)

Tapeats Creek
2440 ft (744 m)

4000 ft (1219 m)

Colorado River
2000 ft (610 m)

Surprise Valley Junction
3800 ft (1158 m)

3000 ft (914 m)

Deer Creek Trail/Deer Creek & Spring
2400 ft (732 m)

THUNDER RIVER TRAIL

Trailhead
The Thunder River Trail begins at Indian Hollow. To reach it, follow Highway 67 to Forest Service (FS) road 422 west toward Dry Park. Then take FS425 to FS232. To reach the Bill Hall trailhead at Monument Point, follow Highway 67 to FS422 west. Then take FS425 to FS292 and continue west along the rim on FS292A. The trail begins 0.5 mile (0.8 km) from the end of the road.

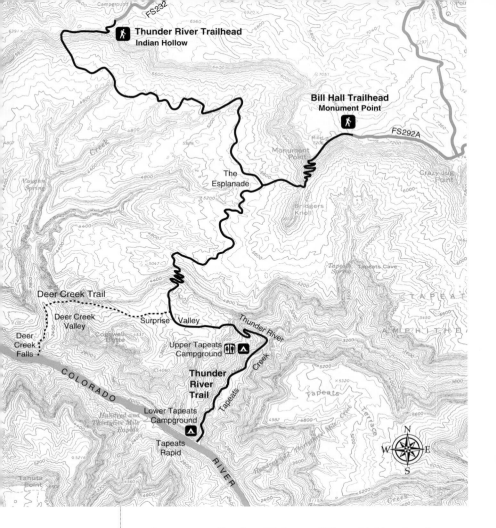

Crews normally plow Highway 67 by mid-May, but forest roads may not be open until June. Roads usually close again in early November.

Route

After leaving the parking area at Indian Hollow, the Thunder River Trail descends westward through the upper cliffs until reaching the broad Esplanade terrace. The trail turns east, covering about 4 miles (6.4 km) until joining the Monument Point route.

The Monument Point route (Bill Hall Trail) descends steeply through the Kaibab and Toroweap Formations before leading to a break on the west side of the point. The route can be difficult with a pack, requiring hands-on

scrambling in places. Stay on the footpath, clearly marked with cairns, as it descends a steep talus slope through the Coconino Sandstone. This route merges with the Thunder River Trail from Indian Hollow and continues south-southwest along the Esplanade for several miles. Cairns mark the route.

After passing several drainages, the trail descends the Redwall Limestone into Surprise Valley. The route continues east to Thunder River, crossing several washes and rolling hills. Steep switchbacks lead past Thunder River, plunging down a 100-foot (30m) cliff in a dramatic waterfall. Reaching the confluence with Tapeats Creek, the trail continues downstream below Upper Tapeats Campground. The pathway crosses the creek twice and bypasses the deep lower gorge on the west side before reaching the Colorado River.

above:
Rattlesnake.

opposite:
Waterfall along
Thunder River
near Tapeats Creek.

below:
Deer Creek Narrows.

Variation

Once in Surprise Valley, the **Deer Creek Trail** branches west (right) into Deer Creek Valley. Entering a deep narrows, the trail traverses a ledge on the west side. Leaving the narrows, it descends a talus slope to the base of the waterfall and the Colorado River.

NORTH BASS TRAIL

Maps:

Powell Plateau
(15 minute)

King Arthur Castle
Havasupai Point
(7.5 minute)

Length
• about 14 miles (22.5 km): North Bass trailhead to the Colorado River

Elevations
• 7500 feet (2286 m): North Bass trailhead (Swamp Point)
• 2200 feet (671 m): Colorado River

Water Sources
• Muav Spring (seasonal)
• White Creek (perennial but intermittent)
• Shinumo Creek
• Colorado River

Trail Conditions
Wilderness Trail. Washouts, rockslides, and heavy brush require considerable route-finding skill. One of the canyon's most strenuous trails. Prior Grand Canyon hiking experience strongly recommended.

Trailhead
From Highway 67 head west on Forest Service (FS) road 422, an all-weather logging road. At the top of the ridge take FS270, turning right (west) onto FS223. Turn left (south) on FS268 and bear left on FS268B. Turn right (west) at the intersection with the Swamp Point Road. Road conditions deteriorate on the last ten miles from the park boundary to Swamp Point. High clearance, four-wheel drive vehicles are recommended. Roads may not be cleared of snow and winter treefall until early June.

North Bass Trailhead/Swamp Point
7500 ft (2286 m)

Muav Saddle Cabin
6760 ft (2060 m)   7000 ft (2134 m)

Enter Muav Canyon/White Creek
5640 ft (1719 m)   6000 ft (1829 m)

Bass Rapids
2200 ft (671 m)   5000 ft (1524 m)

Shinumo Falls
2400 ft (732 m)   4000 ft (1219 m)

Shinumo Camp
2480 ft (756 m)   3000 ft (914 m)

NORTH BASS TRAIL

Route
From Swamp Point, the trail descends a series of switchbacks to a trail junction in Muav Saddle. The right branch goes to an old cabin and the middle leads to Powell Plateau. The North Bass Trail leaves the saddle by the left branch, traversing east along the base of the Coconino Sandstone. Before you reach Muav Saddle Spring, a cairn marks the descent route into White Canyon down a talus ridge. The route meanders down the steep talus to a dry branch of upper White Creek that soon joins the main drainage.

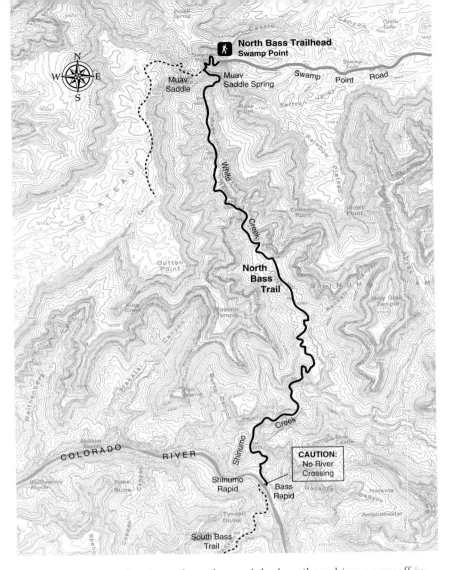

North Bass Trailhead
Swamp Point

Muav
Saddle

Muav
Saddle Spring

Swamp Point Road

White

Creek

North
Bass
Trail

Creek

Shinumo

COLORADO   RIVER

Shinumo
Rapid

Bass
Rapid

CAUTION:
No River
Crossing

South Bass
Trail

NOTE:
Camping along
the Colorado River
at the foot of the
trail is off-limits to
backpackers.

Continue along the creek bed until reaching a pouroff in the Redwall cliff. The trail climbs out of the creek bed on the right (west) and contours above the rim of the Redwall gorge. Heavy brush can make the trail difficult to follow. Stay on the bypass as it crosses two ravines and enters a third for a short distance. Leaving the third ravine, the trail contours along the base of the rimrock cliff to the Redwall descent. Switchbacks lead through the Redwall Limestone to White Creek.

Head downstream until reaching a pouroff in the Bright Angel Shale. A bypass to the right (west) leads to the Tonto

right: Bass built a tramway (now dismantled) to transport visitors across the Colorado River.

When his doctor gave William Bass only a few years to live, Bass headed west in a desperate attempt to regain his health. He made friends with Havasupai Indians who guided him into remote parts of the canyon where he began developing several mines.

The trails Bass constructed to these claims proved valuable when his tourist business grew. The guide built a camp along Shinumo Creek with orchards and a garden to supply his family and tourist operation on the South Rim.

Bass outlived his doctor's prediction by half a century.

Platform and loops back to the creek bed. The trail stays in the main drainage until reaching another pouroff in the Tapeats narrows.

The standard route bypasses this drop to the left (east) and works its way back to White Creek down a side canyon. An old horse trail, without water or shade, leaves the creek bed on the right (west) and crosses the Tonto Platform to Shinumo Creek. The standard route follows White Creek through the Tapeats narrows until reaching a pouroff in the Vishnu Schist. Bypass to the left (east) and continue a short distance to Shinumo Creek. Turn downstream and be prepared for a number of wet crossings. High spring runoff may prevent wading across the stream. An alternate route follows the right (west) side above the creek.

The trail winds down Shinumo until about 1 mile (1.6 km) above the river where it climbs left (south) 500 feet (152 m) up a talus slope. After crossing a high ridge, it descends to the Colorado River upriver from the mouth of Shinumo Creek.

above: William Bass (left) and friends at Shinumo Camp.

right: Artifacts at Shinumo Camp, North Bass Trail.

NOTE: *Historic artifacts, protected by law, remain along Shinumo Creek from the Bass occupation of the area. Leave them for the enjoyment of others.*

NORTH KAIBAB TRAIL

Maps:

Bright Angel (15 minute)

Bright Angel Point Phantom Ranch (7.5 minute)

Indians and prospectors originally used a route now followed by the Old Kaibab Trail.

Mapmaker Francois Matthes improved the trail during his Grand Canyon survey in 1902. A year later, David Rust established a tourist camp at the mouth of Bright Angel Creek.

Rust constructed a cable crossing over the Colorado River a few years later, linking the North and South Rims. The Fred Harvey Company acquired Rust's holdings and built Phantom Ranch, a tourist lodge named after nearby Phantom Creek.

Length
- 4.7 miles (7.6 km): North Kaibab trailhead to Roaring Springs
- 6.8 miles (11 km): North Kaibab trailhead to Cottonwood Campground
- 14.2 miles (22.9 km): North Kaibab trailhead to the Colorado River

Elevations
- 8250 feet (2515 m): North Kaibab trailhead
- 5200 feet (1585 m): Roaring Springs
- 4080 feet (1244 m): Cottonwood Campground
- 2400 feet (732 m): Colorado River

Water Sources
- Roaring Springs
- Bright Angel Creek
- Cottonwood Campground (May through October)
- Bright Angel Campground
- Colorado River

Trail Conditions
Corridor Trail. Regularly maintained and well marked.

Trailhead
North Kaibab Trail begins on the North Entrance Road, about 2 miles (3.2 km) north of Grand Canyon Lodge and about 11 miles (17.7 km) south of the entrance station.

above:
Fall foliage
along upper
North Kaibab Trail.

right:
Ribbon Falls,
North Kaibab Trail.

NOTE:
The North Rim and
the North Kaibab
Trail remain closed
from mid-November
to mid-May because
of heavy snowfall.

The North Rim can
be reached during
winter by experi-
enced cross-country
skiers willing to
undertake a
strenuous 45-mile
(72 km) trip from
Jacob Lake. A
backcountry permit
is required.

NORTH RIM

Ken Patrick Trail

North Kaibab Trailhead

Uncle Jim Trail

Old Bright Angel Route

Supai Tunnel

Widforss Trail

Grand Canyon Lodge

Bright Angel Point

Roaring Springs

Cottonwood Camp (summer only)

Ribbon Falls

North Kaibab Trail

Clear Creek Trail

Phantom Ranch

Bright Angel Campground

Bright Angel Trail

South Kaibab Trail

COLORADO RIVER

Route

The trail descends steeply for the first 4.7 miles (7.6 km) to the junction of Roaring Springs Canyon and Bright Angel Creek. The trail gradient lessens as it follows Bright Angel past Cottonwood Campground (closed during winter months). A spur trail to Ribbon Falls branches off about 1 mile (1.6 km) below the campground. You can cross the creek on a footbridge.

The main trail continues down Bright Angel Canyon, passing through a 1200-foot (366 m) deep inner gorge called The Box. Just beyond Phantom Ranch, the trail reaches Bright Angel Campground near the Colorado River.

NOTE:
Guided mule trips use the upper section of the North Kaibab Trail. Mules have the right of way. When a mule string passes, stand quietly to the inside of the trail and obey instructions from the wrangler.

right:
Bright Angel Campground.

Variation

Old Bright Angel Route, 7.8 miles (12.6 km) long. The trail can be reached from the North Kaibab trailhead by following the Ken Patrick Trail. Good route-finding skills are required for this unmaintained route.

The old trail descends a series of steep switchbacks in the upper canyon cliffs. Scrub oak thickets obscure the upper portion of the trail, but conditions improve as it descends. The trail bypasses a pouroff at the top of the Redwall cliff by climbing to the right (west) and leading to a steep break. After reaching Bright Angel Creek, the trail stays above the creek bed on the west side to avoid brush and boulders. About 0.5 mile (0.8 km) before reaching the junction with Roaring Springs Canyon, the trail crosses to the east side.

CLEAR CREEK TRAIL

Maps:

Bright Angel
Vishnu Temple
(15 minute)

Phantom Ranch
(7.5 minute)

The Civilian
Conservation Corps
built the trail to
Clear Creek in 1933.

The northeast arm
of Clear Creek
Canyon, north of
Honan Point,
contains the highest
waterfall in Grand
Canyon. Most times
of the year, Cheyava
Falls is a mere
trickle, but after a
wet winter it gushes
from the cliff face in
a series of cascades.

Length
- 8.7 miles (14 km): Clear Creek trailhead to Clear Creek

Elevations
- 2640 feet (805 m): Clear Creek trailhead
- 4160 feet (1268 m): Tonto Platform
- 3440 feet (1049 m): Clear Creek

Water Sources
- Bright Angel Creek
- Clear Creek

Trail Conditions
Wilderness Trail. Route finding is not difficult.

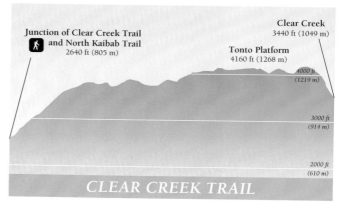

Trailhead
Clear Creek Trail leaves the North Kaibab Trail 0.3 mile (0.5 km) north of Phantom Ranch.

Route
Leaving Bright Angel Creek, the trail switchbacks up a talus slope to the base of Sumner Butte. Contouring around the corner, the trail ascends a break to the Tonto Platform. The trail follows the Tonto for most of its length, turning north and staying above Clear Creek for some distance before descending to the stream bed.

Variations
To River: A day hike down Clear Creek to the river involves frequent stream crossings. A climb is required to bypass a 15-foot (4.6 m) pouroff, 0.25 mile (0.40 km) from the river.
Cheyava Falls: To reach seasonal (snowmelt-fed) Cheyava Falls, follow Clear Creek north from Clear Creek Campground for 5 miles. Several stream crossings are required; there is no established trail.

The Kolb brothers, early canyon photographers, first explored Cheyava Falls in 1903 after a prospector spotted what he thought was a cliff coated with a sheet of ice.

right:
Cheyava Falls,
1910.

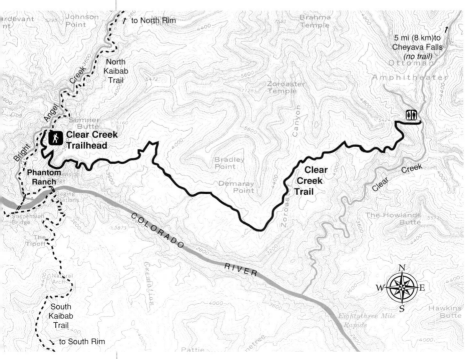

NANKOWEAP TRAIL

Maps:

Nankoweap (15 minute)

Point Imperial Nankoweap Mesa (7.5 minute)

In 1882, canyon explorer and geologist John Wesley Powell directed the building of a trail into Nankoweap Valley that followed a Paiute route. His colleague, geologist Charles Walcott, used it to reach isolated rock formations in the eastern Grand Canyon.

Length
- 14.5 miles (23.3 km): FS610 road-head to Colorado River
- 14 miles (22.5 km): FS445 road-head to Colorado River
- 11 miles (17.7 km): National Park Service trailhead (Saddle Mountain saddle) to Colorado River

Elevations
- 8800 feet (2682 m): FS Trail 57 at FS610 roadhead
- 7560 feet (2304 m): National Park Service trailhead at Saddle Mountain Saddle
- 2760 feet (841 m): Colorado River

Water Sources
- Nankoweap Creek
- Colorado River

Trail Conditions
Wilderness Trail. Washouts and rock-fall require some route-finding skill. One of the canyon's most strenuous trails. Not recommended for inexperienced or solo hikers.

Trailhead
The trailheads can be accessed from the west via Forest Service (FS) road 610, or from the north through House Rock Valley via FS445. FS445 is a lower elevation access and more reliable year-round. NOTE that both trailheads are called Saddle Mountain and that both Forest Service trails are numbered 57.

Route
From the FS610 roadhead, go 3.5 miles (5.6 km) on Forest Service Trail 57 to the National Park Service trailhead on the canyon rim. This leg of the trail is straightforward but brushy in places. The route

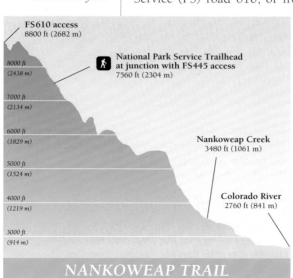

Profile labels:
FS610 access
8800 ft (2682 m)

National Park Service Trailhead at junction with FS445 access
7560 ft (2304 m)

8000 ft (2438 m)
7000 ft (2134 m)
6000 ft (1829 m)
5000 ft (1524 m)
4000 ft (1219 m)
3000 ft (914 m)

Nankoweap Creek
3480 ft (1061 m)

Colorado River
2760 ft (841 m)

NANKOWEAP TRAIL

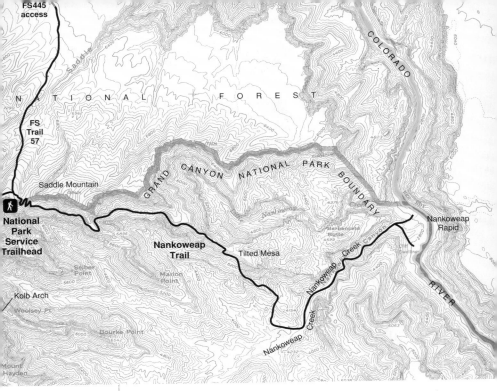

Kolb Arch, the largest natural bridge in the canyon, is found in an upper arm of Nankoweap Canyon below Woolsey Point.

Ellsworth and Emery Kolb, 1929.

from the FS445 roadhead in House Rock Valley reaches the NPS trailhead via the 3-mile (4.8-km) continuation of FS Trail 57.

From the canyon rim, the Nankoweap Trail drops to a ledge in the Supai cliffs and contours eastward a number of miles to Tilted Mesa. The trail narrows to the width of a foot-step in a few places where drop-offs exceed 100 feet (30m).

Following the ridge that leads down to Tilted Mesa, the trail descends a number of stairstep ledges in the Supai that require hand-and-foot scrambles. The trail reaches the Red-wall along a narrow neck separating Nankoweap and Little Nankoweap Canyons.

The route descends steep sections of the Redwall and Muav Limestones and the Bright Angel Shale on hard-packed slopes coated with loose scree. Trail construction can be seen in places, but most of the old trail washed into the gorge long ago. Heavy rains continue to erode the route. After switchbacking through the Tapeats Sandstone and past the dark Nankoweap and Cardenas Formations, the trail crosses a large alluvial terrace above the creek. Reaching Nankoweap Creek, the trail turns downstream and continues to the river.

SUGGESTED READING

INDIVIDUAL TRAIL GUIDES

Grand Canyon Association has published a set of individual pocket-size trail guides that include information about the human and natural history of the park's most popular trails, as well as providing route-finding information and maps. Guides are available for the following trails:

• *Bass Trail, North & South* by Jim Babbitt & Scott Thybony
• *Bright Angel Trail* by Alan Berkowitz
• *Grandview Trail* by John Good
• *Havasu Canyon Trail* by Scott Thybony
• *Hermit Trail* by Scott Thybony
• *North Kaibab Trail* by Alan Berkowitz
• *South Kaibab Trail* by Rose Houk

ADDITIONAL TRAIL GUIDES

Annerino, John. *Hiking the Grand Canyon*. A Sierra Club Totebook; comprehensive guide to planning and executing a hike at the Grand Canyon. Small to fit well in backpack.

Butchart, Harvey. *Butchart Grand Canyon Treks: 12,000 Miles Through the Grand Canyon.* Concise guides to off-trail routes and lesser-known trails in the backcountry wilderness. Written by a legendary canyon hiker who has walked thousands of miles below the rim.

MAPS

Bright Angel Trail Hiking Map and Guide, Earthwalk Press. Full color topographic map (scale 1:24,000) with trail designations and computer terrain models. Covers Bright Angel Canyon (Bright Angel, South Kaibab, and North Kaibab Trails only).

Grand Canyon National Park, Trails Illustrated Topo Maps. Full color topographic map (scale approximately 1:73,530) with trail designations. Covers North and South Rim trails from river mile 1 (Lees Ferry) to river mile 173 (west of Havasu Canyon). Printed on waterproof, tearproof plastic.

Hiking Map and Guide, Grand Canyon National Park, Earthwalk Press. Full color topographic map (scale 1:48,000) with trail designations. Covers Hermit Trail to Grandview Trail (including North Kaibab Trail).

OTHER SUBJECTS OF INTEREST

Anderson, Michael F. *Along the Rim: A Guide to Grand Canyon's South Rim from Hermits Rest to Desert View*. A road guide to the South Rim with a focus on its pioneer history.

Coder, Christopher M. *An Introduction to Grand Canyon Prehistory*. An introduction to Grand Canyon archaeology, examining the people who have inhabited the canyon during the past twelve thousand years.

Fletcher, Colin. *The Man Who Walked Through Time*. A classic personal account of the first documented journey on foot through most of Grand Canyon.

Houk, Rose. *An Introduction to Grand Canyon Ecology*. A guide to the many life zones found at Grand Canyon and the plants and animals that inhabit them.

Price, L. Greer. *An Introduction to Grand Canyon Geology*. An overview of Grand Canyon geology written for the lay reader. Includes many photographs and illustrations.

Schmidt, Jeremy. *Grand Canyon National Park, A Natural History Guide*. A comprehensive look at the geology and the ecosystems of the canyon.

Thybony, Scott. *Phantom Ranch*. A guide to Phantom Ranch, an oasis found at the bottom of the canyon. Includes sections on the ranch's history, plants, animals, and the people who live there.

All titles are available through:

GRAND CANYON ASSOCIATION
P. O. Box 399,
Grand Canyon, AZ
86023-0399

Telephone: 520-638-2481
Fax: 520-638-2484
www.grandcanyon.org

GEOLOGIC CROSS SECTION
OF THE GRAND CANYON

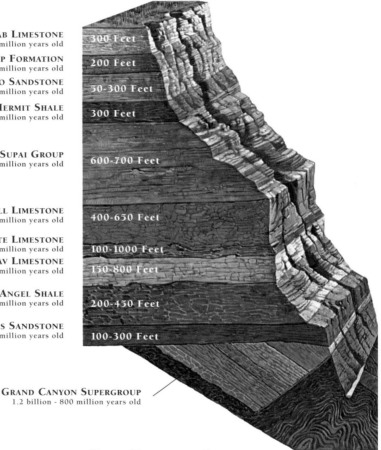

KAIBAB LIMESTONE
250 million years old

300 Feet

TOROWEAP FORMATION
260 million years old

200 Feet

COCONINO SANDSTONE
270 million years old

50-300 Feet

HERMIT SHALE
280 million years old

300 Feet

SUPAI GROUP
300 million years old

600-700 Feet

REDWALL LIMESTONE
330 million years old

400-650 Feet

TEMPLE BUTTE LIMESTONE
370 million years old

100-1000 Feet

MUAV LIMESTONE
530 million years old

150-800 Feet

BRIGHT ANGEL SHALE
540 million years old

200-450 Feet

TAPEATS SANDSTONE
550 million years old

100-300 Feet

GRAND CANYON SUPERGROUP
1.2 billion - 800 million years old

VISHNU METAMORPHIC COMPLEX
1.7 billion years old